ENGINEERING WONDERS OF THE 21ST C[...]

I0893122

Great SHIP Designs

BY SOPHIE WASHBURNE

Cavendish Square
NEW YORK

Published in 2023 by Cavendish Square Publishing, LLC
29 East 21st Street, New York, NY 10010

Copyright © 2023 by Cavendish Square Publishing, LLC

No part of this publication may be reproduced, stored in a retrieval system, or transmitted in any form or by any means—electronic, mechanical, photocopying, recording, or otherwise—without the prior permission of the copyright owner. Request for permission should be addressed to Permissions, Cavendish Square Publishing, 29 East 21st Street, New York, NY 10010. Tel (877) 980-4450; fax (877) 980-4454.

Website: cavendishsq.com

Disclaimer: Portions of this work were originally authored by Philip Wolny and published as *21st-Century Ships*. All new material this edition authored by Sophie Washburne.

This publication represents the opinions and views of the author based on his or her personal experience, knowledge, and research. The information in this book serves as a general guide only. The author and publisher have used their best efforts in preparing this book and disclaim liability rising directly or indirectly from the use and application of this book.

All websites were available and accurate when this book was sent to press.

Library of Congress Cataloging-in-Publication Data
Names: Washburne, Sophie, author.
Title: Great ship designs / by Sophie Washburne.
Description: New York, NY : Cavendish Square Publishing, [2023] | Series: Engineering wonders of the 21st century | Includes index.
Identifiers: LCCN 2021056544 | ISBN 9781502665164 (library binding) | ISBN 9781502665157 (paperback) | ISBN 9781502665171 (ebook)
Subjects: LCSH: Ships--Juvenile literature. | Shipbuilding--Juvenile literature. | Ships--Environmental aspects--Juvenile literature. | CYAC: Ships.
Classification: LCC VM150 .W35 2023 | DDC 623.82--dc23/eng/20211209
LC record available at https://lccn.loc.gov/2021056544

Editor: Jennifer Lombardo
Copyeditor: Michelle Denton
Designer: Rachel Rising

The photographs in this book are used by permission and through the courtesy of: Cover, NAN728/Shutterstock.com; cover, pp. 1–48 (gears) Artistdesign29/Shutterstock.com; cover, pp. 1–48 (grid) Cesar Termulo Jr/Shutterstock.com; cover, pp. 1–48 (boxes) Olessia_Art/Shutterstock.com; p. 4 TravelSH/Shutterstock.com; p. 6 https://commons.wikimedia.org/wiki/File:SS_La_Touraine.jpg; p. 7 Shinonome Production/Shutterstock.com; p. 8 DC Studio/Shutterstock.com; p. 11 Khrushchev Georgy/Shutterstock.com; p. 12 Designua/Shutterstock.com; p. 15 Xinhua/Alamy Stock Photo; p. 16 Yongyut Kumsri/Shutterstock.com; p. 19 Mia2you/Shutterstock.com; p. 20 AliveGK/Shutterstock.com; p. 22 Alexey Lesik/Shutterstock.com; p. 23 StockStudio Aerials/Shutterstock.com; p. 24 Oliver Hoffmann/Shutterstock.com; p. 26 Tigergallery/Shutterstock.com; p. 28 Avigator Fortuner/Shutterstock.com; p. 30 Geof Kirby/Alamy Stock Photo; p. 31 Serge Prakhov/Shutterstock.com; p. 32 Asar Studios/Alamy Stock Photo; p. 34 Mike Shamon/Shutterstock.com; p. 36 Jan Miko/Shutterstock.com; p. 38 dpa picture alliance archive/Alamy Stock Photo; p. 40 VectorMine/Shutterstock.com; p. 42 Bob Daemmrich Alamy Stock Photo.

Some of the images in this book illustrate individuals who are models.
The depictions do not imply actual situations or events.

CPSIA compliance information: Batch #CSCSQ23: For further information contact Cavendish Square Publishing LLC, New York, New York, at 1-877-980-4450.

Printed in the United States of America

Find us on

CONTENTS

Introduction

Traveling on the seas has been an important human activity for thousands of years. For most of history, boats and ships were the only way to cross long distances over water. The earliest example of a boat that experts have found dates back to 4000 BCE in ancient Egypt. It had sails, but it also had oars because the winds on the Nile River were unpredictable.

This ancient Egyptian ship was found buried at the foot of the Great Pyramid of Giza.

When Egyptians started exploring the Mediterranean Sea, they had to change the design of their boat to make it a ship. One main difference between a boat and a ship is that a boat is made to travel in smaller bodies of water, such as rivers and lakes, while a ship is designed to sail on the open ocean. This is part of why ships are so much bigger than boats.

Ship design did not change much until the Industrial Revolution of the 18th and 19th centuries. When steam power became available, it was first used on ships because the steam engines were huge. Ships could be made bigger to fit the engine in a way trains and other vehicles could not. Steamboats were developed in 1807, and in 1809, an experimenter named John Stevens used a steamboat to make an ocean trip between New Jersey and Delaware. From there, things progressed quickly, and the first ocean crossing made by a steamship took place in 1818. As technology has continued to advance, steamships have been improved.

Some people believe we do not need ships anymore because we have faster ways of traveling, such as airplanes. However, ships are important because they still move goods and people around the world. In 2021, it became clear how much the world still relies on ships to move many goods. At the start of the COVID-19 pandemic in 2020, demand for shipping fell.

Steamships, often called steamers, were the best way to get people and goods across oceans in the 1800s and early 1900s.

However, by the end of the year, demand grew again so quickly that companies could not keep up. Traffic jams in ports around the world, as well as a shortage of workers who could pack and unload the items, caused delays and increased expenses on all kinds of items, from electronics to candy.

The demand for bigger and better ships grows every year, and not only for ships that carry goods. Cruise line companies love to launch increasingly impressive cruise ships. Navies around the world want more advanced ships. Scientists use ships to do certain kinds of research.

Land vehicles can get only so big, but ocean vessels can keep increasing in size. On the ocean, the only limit for a ship is whether an engine can power it. This is why engineers are always working on creating more **efficient** engines for ships.

Today, computers are an important part of making and running ships.

CAD software can help engineers picture all parts of a design before it is built. This makes it easier to identify and fix problems.

CHAPTER ONE

Safety First

Since ships spend most of their time on the open ocean, they must be seaworthy. This means they have to be protected against leaks, and they must be able to navigate rough waters and occasional storms. Ships need careful planning and testing before they can go out on open water. If a car breaks down on the highway, it can be towed to a mechanic, and it's often nothing more than an inconvenience for the driver and passengers (although sometimes an expensive one). However, if a ship has problems in the ocean, hundreds of miles from shore, it puts the whole crew in serious danger.

STARTING WITH AN IDEA

Shipbuilding is an incredible process. It starts with basic designs and engineering plans. Today, these are generally done using computer-aided design (CAD). A good design is the difference between ships that are seaworthy and those that sink or break down. People who design and build ships are sometimes known as naval architects. Just as land architects oversee the process of making buildings, naval architects oversee shipbuilding.

Once a ship's designs are approved, the next stage is production planning. Big companies, including car companies such as Hyundai and Mitsubishi, manufacture most large vessels. The production process includes many different people, and plans are often reviewed and revised many times.

With plans finalized, shipbuilders prepare a facility for the new construction. This construction typically takes place at a shipyard. For very big ships, the shipbuilders use steel to build most or all of the outside of the ship, which is called the hull. When steel is exposed to water for long periods of time, it **corrodes**. This is why the steel of the hull needs to be sealed with special chemicals.

Building ships the way we do today would not have been possible before the Industrial Revolution because it requires so many machines. After the steel is treated to prevent corrosion, workers run giant machines to turn huge pieces of steel into smaller sheets. Different machines are used to roll sheets of steel into the shapes needed to build the hull and other parts of the ship. Still other machines build the structures that will fill the inside of the ship.

Many ships are built using a process called the hull block construction method. Because ships are so huge, they are built in parts, or blocks, and then those blocks are added to the main hull later. This makes it easier for workers to fit pipes and other equipment in each block. The workers assemble the hull blocks in a carefully planned order on a shipbuilding dock.

Shown here are two workers welding pieces onto a ship.

The Science of Ships

Scientists have studied how water behaves for thousands of years. In the Western world, the Greek mathematician Archimedes is credited with first writing about the concept of buoyancy around 250 BCE. Buoyancy is the force a fluid has as it pushes up against something that has been placed in it. For example, Archimedes claimed that he experimented by dropping a crown in water. He then calculated how much water was displaced, or moved, by that crown. Try to pick up a heavy object underwater. You will notice that it feels lighter than it would on dry land. This is because the buoyant force of the water is helping you a bit.

The more a boat weighs, the more it tends to sink in the water. However, the air inside a boat is less dense less than the water, which is what keeps it up. When the weight of the boat is less than or equal to the amount of the water it displaces, it floats. This is because the water pushes back on the boat with a force that is equal to the weight of the boat.

This diagram shows how displacement works. Notice that when more of an object is underwater, the water rises higher above the red line.

Once everything is put together, it is time to test the ship's seaworthiness. This means the ship is placed in the water to see if it floats without any problems. If the ship is deemed seaworthy, the shipbuilding facility delivers it to the owners that commissioned, or ordered, it.

MANY SHIPS FOR MANY NEEDS

Today, there are many kinds of big ships sailing the seas. Some are passenger vessels. These big ships, such as cruise ships and ferries, carry large numbers of people. A cruise ship is similar to a giant floating hotel. Its crew must be very big to handle the hundreds or even thousands of guests it holds. Other ships, such as oil tankers and container ships that carry cargo, have smaller crews. Tanker design has to account for the way oil and other liquid cargo moves back and forth in transit. Meanwhile, container ships and other cargo vessels have to be able to handle huge differences in weight.

Each kind of ship might be designed in a slightly different way. The differences are important because carrying oil and carrying 1,500 human passengers are two completely different jobs. A warship will often have ultra-thin armor on it to protect against attack but not enough to slow it down. Some ships may even be designed for certain sea routes. For example, certain tankers are too big to make it through important canals, such as the Suez Canal connecting the Persian Gulf with the Mediterranean Sea.

In March 2021, the world saw just how important it was to have the right ship for the right job when the *Ever Given*—one of the largest container ships ever built—got stuck sideways in the Suez Canal. It blocked shipping traffic for six days, leading to delays and billions of dollars lost. Many people pointed out that the ship was much too big for the canal. Its **keel** almost touched the bottom, and it was so wide that when it was blown sideways by strong winds, it got stuck between the canal's banks.

THINK IT THROUGH

1. What kinds of things do naval architects have to think about when designing a ship?
2. Why does a ship need pipes in it?
3. How could people prevent another ship from being stuck in the Suez Canal or a similar waterway?

The *Ever Given* needed to be pushed off the canal banks by smaller boats after large machines dug the dirt away from its keel.

A ship that sails to Antarctica, such as the one shown here, is likely to have a long, pointed **bow** to help it cut through rough waters.

CHAPTER TWO

Moving People and Cargo

Cruise ships became popular in the 1960s as a luxury vacation option. These ships take people to and from the same port, often visiting other ports on the way during a trip of several days. The way a cruise ship is designed sometimes depends on where the cruise takes place. For example, a Caribbean cruise ship may have a short, wide bow because it will not face stormy seas as often as a ship that takes passengers to Antarctica.

THE SYMPHONY OF THE SEAS

The *Symphony of the Seas*, which is owned by Royal Caribbean International, is the largest cruise ship in the world as of 2021. Ship size is often judged by gross tonnage (GT), and the *Symphony* measures a staggering 228,081 GT. It is 1,188 feet (362 meters) long and 238 feet (72.5 m) tall. This size

A Well-Known Tragedy

Not long ago, there was not really a cruise ship industry. Instead, boats of that size were known as ocean liners. Such ships were used mainly for crossing between Europe and the Americas in a time before airplanes could take many passengers. They were built with reinforced steel that was supposed to help them meet any challenge on the high seas. The bow was tapered. This helped the liner cut through high or heavy waves. The most famous ocean liner ever built was the *Titanic*. The builders of the *Titanic* claimed that it was impossible to sink, but it sank on its very first trip in 1912.

There are several reasons why the *Titanic* tragedy happened. One is that the captain was eager to make the crossing take as little time as possible. Because the ship was moving so fast, its collision with an iceberg ripped a hole in the hull, causing the ship to sink. No one had expected this, so there were not enough lifeboats on board to save everyone. People learned from this tragedy, so today, ships need to have a certain number of lifeboats even if the ship has successfully made many trips.

makes it seem like a small floating city. There is room for a 10-story water slide, laser tag arena, theater, spa, helicopter pad, and much more.

A ship of this size needs plenty of power in the engine room to move it. The *Symphony*'s three ABB Azipod thrusters, which push it along underwater, use what are basically giant propellers. Each is powered by an electric drive motor located in a pod outside the hull. Additional thrusters—sometimes known as tunnel thrusters—are often built into the bow or **stern** of a cruise ship. These help ships such as the *Symphony* maneuver, especially when doing trickier moves such as **docking** at a port.

The *Symphony of the Seas* has 18 decks and room for 9,000 people, counting both passengers and crew. For comparison, the population of Sedona, Arizona, is about 10,000.

If something goes wrong with the engines on a ship, the crew needs to know about it immediately. Computers help them monitor the engines. Shown here is the engine surveillance system on the *Symphony of the Seas*.

All this power means cruise ships use up a lot of fuel. The engines on the *Harmony of the Seas*, which was the biggest cruise ship until 2017, can burn 66,000 gallons (300,042 liters) of fuel per day at full power—and they actually use about 20 percent less power than earlier Royal Caribbean models. There are ways to make cruise ships more fuel-efficient and more environmentally-friendly. Some of the features on the *Harmony* include the following:

- Air bubbles that are naturally forced out of the hull help the ship ride more easily through the water, meaning the ship needs to use less power to keep it moving.
- Better insulation keeps heat and air-conditioning in and outside heat or cold out.

- Heat created by the engines powers steam generators.
- Self-cleaning systems in the engines called gas scrubbers get rid of up to 98 percent of some kinds of dangerous air-polluting gases.
- Light-emitting diodes (LEDs) are installed all over the ship. LED lights use less energy, work for much longer, and are believed to be safer for the environment when thrown away.

New technologies being developed now—and future ones we can't even imagine—will make even more incredible cruise ships possible. Modern engineers imagine using super-strong alloys, or combinations of steel and other metals, that are also super lightweight. Those who care about the environment are working on ways to power cruise ships with solar or wind power. Some people picture cruise ships getting bigger and bigger until they actually do resemble cities floating around the world.

MOVING CARGO

Many of the products in stores and homes are shipped from faraway places. While some items are sent by plane, train, or truck, many of them got to where they were going on a giant cargo ship. A bulk cargo ship carries large amounts of items such as grain or other crops, gravel, cement, wood chips, refrigerated goods, animal products, and much more. Such

Shown here is corn being loaded into a bulk cargo ship.

bulk items can be tossed together in large spaces called holds because they do not need to be packed carefully.

Another kind of cargo vessel is the container ship. Toward the end of the 20th century, storage containers became the most important way of shipping non-bulk cargo. Having a predictable container size makes loading and unloading this cargo much quicker. It also requires far fewer human beings on the docks.

Container ships are some of the largest ships on Earth. Many of those launched since the beginning of the 21st century are so big that they can only dock at a small number of ports around the world. Some cannot pass through the Suez or Panama Canals. Even many of those that can need special procedures to do so, such as being pulled by smaller ships called tugboats.

Because cargo ships have so much extra weight on them, they need a special design to spread that weight out evenly on the water. Ballast water is water that is taken into the hull of a ship, helping to balance the ship and make it stable. This helps when a ship's weight changes as containers or other cargo are added or removed. It can be dumped to make the boat lighter when it needs to get through shallow waters. New "ecological" ballast filters and systems remove organisms that are accidentally sucked up from seawater. Many **invasive** water species destroy native ones when they are picked up in one place by ballast water and dumped in another.

GETTING BIGGER AND BIGGER

It seems that hardly a year goes by without another container ship being named the "biggest ship on the high seas." Maersk, the Danish company that is the largest container and cargo operator in the world, introduced its Triple E Class ships in 2013. The

When ships dump their ballast water, any small creatures that were picked up with it are also dumped. These invasive species can take over the habitat of the native species and wipe them out.

Madrid Maersk is 1,309 feet (399 m) long. Shipping containers are 20 feet (6 m) long, so the carrying capacity of a container ship is measured in “twenty-foot equivalent units,” or TEUs. The *Madrid Maersk* has a TEU of 20,568. The Maersk E Class ships use as much steel as eight Eiffel Towers. The containers they hold could fill more than 36,000 cars or 30 trains that are 1 mile (1.6 kilometers) long!

Maersk also says that these ships are the most environmentally friendly container ships ever made. They carry 16 percent more cargo, even though they are only about 9.8 feet (3 m) longer and wider than previous container vessels the company produced. New engine designs that include reusing engine heat to power other ship systems and limiting the speed of the vessels to 26.4 miles per hour (42.5 km per hour, or 24 **knots**) will also help.

However, it did not take long for Maersk’s ships to be surpassed. As of 2021, the largest container ship in the world is the *HMM Algeciras*, which was made by a Korean company—Daewoo Shipbuilding and Marine Engineering (DSME).

The two kayakers in this picture give a better idea of how huge the *HMM Algeciras* is.

It is 1,312 feet (400 m) long and has a TEU of 24,000. It also has many technological advancements that help it meet the environmental regulations put in place by the International Maritime Organization (IMO). With 174 member countries working together to make rules for international waters, the IMO is the maritime version of the United Nations (UN). Like the *Symphony of the Seas*, the *Algeciras* uses scrubbing systems to remove harmful **emissions** from the air. It also has a hull that has been redesigned to help the ship move quickly and easily through the water, as well as a very efficient engine.

The size of ships will not be the only things that will change in the years ahead. Managers of ports and canals are scrambling to find new ways to accommodate these bigger ships. Shipping lanes will have to change too. The uncertain future that climate change brings will also affect how ships operate.

THINK IT THROUGH

1. Why would a long, pointed bow help a cruise ship navigate rough seas better than a short, flat one?
2. Why do we need both bulk cargo ships and container ships?
3. Can you think of other ways to make a cruise ship or cargo ship more environmentally-friendly?

Oil spills are incredibly difficult to clean up.

CHAPTER THREE

Carrying Fuel and Weapons

Ships can carry things besides people and goods to sell. They are also important parts of militaries and the energy industry. These kinds of ships, like cruise ships and cargo ships, need their own special designs.

A tanker is a kind of ship designed to move large amounts of oil, gas, coal, or similar materials. Tankers can be dangerous because a minor fire can cause an explosion. Furthermore, a **breach** in the hull can cause the cargo to spill out and pollute the water. Even small oil spills can cause terrible damage to oceans and coastal areas. The threat of oil spills led to the passage of laws to make tankers safer. For example, by 2015, all tankers in U.S. waters were required to have a double hull. Like an inner tube inside a car tire, this design helps lessen the risk of major spills. If a breach occurs, the "hull within a hull" at least provides a second line of defense.

BIG SHIPS FOR BIG JOBS

Tankers jumped in size between the 1960s and the 1970s. Making fewer trips is more efficient, which keeps costs down, so companies try to carry as much as they can in one trip. Naval architects of the last few decades have been able to use design software and other technologies to solve shipbuilding problems quickly. These tools also made it easier to efficiently engineer these particular ocean giants.

Because fuel does not come in convenient, standardized sizes the way shipping containers do, tankers do not use TEUs as a measure of carrying capacity. Instead, they use deadweight tonnage (DWT). Tankers have gotten so big that the largest

Oil and gas are in very high demand, so many of these huge tankers sail across the oceans every day.

modern vessels are called supertankers. These are split into two groups: Very Large Crude Carriers (VLCC), which can move from 200,000 to 320,000 DWT, and Ultra Large Crude Carriers (ULCC), which range from 320,000 to 500,000 DWT. They are the world's largest shipping vessels. "Crude" refers to crude oil, which is the kind of oil found underground and in the oceans, before it has been changed into gasoline.

Some of the largest supertankers operating today are four ships built by the company Tankers International in 2002 and 2003: TI Africa, TI Asia, TI Europe, and TI Oceania. These are all 1,247 feet (380 m) long, with about 400,000 DWT. They are known for being very quick for their size; they can go about 19 miles per hour (30.5 km per hour, or 16.5 knots). When gas prices are high, many big ships go slower to save fuel. When prices are low, companies can afford to sail the tankers faster.

A SHIP OR A FLOATING FACTORY?

Perhaps the largest man-made machine of all time is also the largest seagoing vessel. Developed and built by the international energy giant Royal Dutch Shell, the *Prelude FLNG* is a mobile natural gas facility. Some people question whether *Prelude* can truly be considered a vehicle, because although it is built for the water, it is made to stay in one spot for long periods of time.

The Largest Ship Ever Built

The *Seawise Giant* was a supertanker that was built in 1979 by a Japanese company. It was 1,500 feet (457 m) long, with a DWT of about 564,000—the largest in history. The ship was so big that it could not fit through the English Channel or the Suez Canal, and when it started to slow down, it needed to travel 5 miles (8 km) before it could come to a complete stop. Because the ship was so big, all the parts that made it up were also huge. The **rudder** alone weighed 230 tons (208 metric tons)—as much as 46 elephants!

In 1988, during the Iran-Iraq War, the *Seawise Giant* was anchored off the coast of Iran when it was hit with Iraqi bombs and sunk. In 1989, it was brought to the surface, fixed up in Singapore, and sent out to sea again. However, its huge size made it difficult to sail, so in 2004, it was permanently docked in the Persian Gulf and became a storage unit for smaller oil tankers. In 2010, the ship was taken apart, and the scrap metal was sold. Its anchor, which weighs 36 tons (33 metric tons), is on display in the Hong Kong Maritime Museum.

The *Seawise Giant* (*shown here*) is the largest ship in history.

Experts say it is more accurately called a barge because it cannot move under its own power. It is about 1,588 feet (484 m) long and 239.5 feet (73 m) wide.

In addition, *Prelude* has also been built to withstand a Category 5 hurricane, including winds of at least 157 miles per hour (253 km per hour). It was built for around $12 billion in Geoje, South Korea. In June 2017, it arrived at the Browse Basin off Australia's coast, where it has been put to work pumping the offshore gas fields where companies cannot put pipes. However, in 2020, *Forbes* magazine reported that the *Prelude* was not working as planned. Safety problems shut it down in January 2020, and the cost of maintaining it is proving to be far more than the vessel is making for Shell.

The *Prelude (shown here)* is more of a floating factory than a true ship.

USING SHIPS FOR DEFENSE

Warships and other military marine craft have been important parts of national defense for centuries. There are many kinds of military craft. Among the biggest are aircraft carriers. These massive ships do more than just transport personnel and serve as floating airfields. They also allow the military to move large amounts of equipment to conflict zones. The main job of aircraft carriers is to carry fighter jets and other aircraft. Without them, navies and other military branches would have to build or use pre-existing airfields on land. The 21st-century aircraft carrier has some of the most advanced **radar** and networking technologies available.

Aircraft carriers have an angled surface that acts as a runway to help planes take off and land. Shown here is an aircraft carrier with several military planes on it.

As of early 2022, the biggest aircraft carrier in the world belongs to the U.S. fleet. It is the *USS Gerald R. Ford*, the first of a series of ships with the same name. It can carry up to 75 aircraft and 4,539 people. Like all the aircraft carriers built by the U.S. military for some time now, its main power source is not fossil fuel. Rather, it is nuclear-powered. This means that an onboard nuclear facility generates energy. It heats up the steam that powers the **turbines** that help move the ship. It also powers all the other systems. The *Gerald R. Ford* was originally set to launch in 2018, but delays and problems with its technology pushed that date back to 2022.

BATTLESHIP: NOT JUST A BOARD GAME

Aircraft carriers themselves do not fight directly on the open seas. That job is instead left to naval destroyers. While aircraft carriers are bigger and slower, destroyers are swift and easy to **maneuver**. Up through 1945—the final year of World War II—larger battleships handled the jobs that destroyers now handle. Besides fighting other battleships at sea, they had so much firepower that they were used to attack coastlines and other large targets.

Huge battleships went out of style because they were too expensive to build, maintain, and crew. Smaller boats and defense systems could do the job of battleships better and more cheaply. However, although destroyers are smaller and quicker, they still have relatively large crews. For instance, the *USS John S. McCain* has 338 crew members.

New technologies are allowing the U.S. military to launch ships that do more with less. For example, the *USS Zumwal*t, the first of its class, was built to be far more efficient than similar ships. First launched in 2013, it remains the largest destroyer in the world as of 2021—about 100 feet (30.5 m) longer than most U.S. destroyers currently in service. However, it only requires a crew of about 160 people. As of 2021, the *Zumwalt* is the most technologically sophisticated warship ever to hit the water.

One advantage the *Zumwalt* has is that its radar signature is much smaller than that of other destroyers. To enemy radar, it looks like a smaller fishing boat. This makes

Shown here is the *USS Zumwalt* alongside a tugboat for size comparison.

it easy for the ship to sneak near enemy shorelines and attack them. According to *Popular Science* magazine, the ship can get especially close because it can operate in shallower water than most ships. Its weapons are more advanced as well. In the old days, sailors had to manually load shells and clear casings from big naval guns. Now, the guns are controlled by a computer in the ship's command center.

Three of the ships in the Zumwalt class are finished, but in 2021, the U.S. Navy announced that it was looking for a way to fit them with bigger, faster missiles—although the hope is that they will never need to be fired. The U.S. Navy believes this can be a kind of warning to enemy countries. The U.S. Navy also hopes that a warning alone will be enough to make countries think twice before attacking the United States.

THINK IT THROUGH

1. Can you think of more ways to prevent oil spills from tankers?
2. Why would a more technologically advanced ship need a smaller crew?
3. What are some of the advantages and disadvantages of computer-controlled weapons?

A ship with an engine can travel much faster than a sailing ship such as this one. However, most modern ships travel at about the speed of sailing ships anyway because it helps them save fuel, so going back to sails would not impact shipping times much.

CHAPTER FOUR

Saving the Planet

As the climate change crisis grows worse, people are looking for ways to make all kinds of transportation better for the environment. Ships are no exception. Most ships today run on fossil fuels. These release gases such as carbon dioxide, which contributes to climate change. In fact, the shipping industry produces about 3 percent of the world's carbon dioxide emissions—about the same as the entire country of Germany. This is why the IMO has issued environmental guidelines for ships.

While looking forward, naval engineers and architects may take some lessons from the past as well. People stopped using wind as the only power source for their ships when efficient engines started to be developed. This is because if the wind is not blowing, the ship cannot move. However, with new technology, ships could use sails and wind turbines to produce electricity to power their motors.

Using the Sun

In 2010, the German company Knierim Yachtbau launched the *MS Tûranor PlanetSolar.* "Tûranor" means "power of the sun" in Elvish, the language J. R. R. Tolkien invented for *The Lord of the Rings.* Designed by the naval architects at LOMOcean Design, this ship is the world's largest solar-powered ship. It is also the first of its kind to sail itself around the world. The *PlanetSolar* is covered in about 5,500 square feet (512 sq m) of solar panels that power the ship's two electric motors. Onboard batteries store the energy the solar panels collect so the boat can still run at night or when it is cloudy. The 8.5 tons (7.7 metric tons) of batteries can run the ship for 72 hours before needing to be recharged. At that point, they take 48 hours to fully recharge.

Its maximum speed is 14 knots, or 16 miles per hour (25.7 km per hour), but it generally cruises along at 5 knots, or almost 6 miles per hour (9 km per hour). The ship currently acts as a floating laboratory to study climate change on the seas. There is room for a crew of 9, but when it is docked, the boat can accommodate up to 60 passengers.

The *PlanetSolar* can extend its solar panels, as shown here, to get extra power while it is sailing. It is much smaller than many other ships in service today.

GETTING RID OF EMISSIONS

The problem with big ships, even if they are environmentally friendlier now, is emissions. Norway is on the cutting edge of this issue with several inventions. One is a ship called the *Yara Birkeland*, which its designer, a company called Yara International, says is the first zero-emission, fully electric cargo ship. It is also autonomous, or self-driving. On its test trip in 2021, a small crew was on board to make sure there were no problems. Future trips will have no crew at all. Instead, the boat will be controlled and monitored from three onshore data control centers. Another Norwegian company called Zeabuz has created autonomous electric ferries, hoping to help people travel easily while reducing the number of cars on the road.

Some ideas are still in development as of 2021. One of these is a ship called ZERO, which would run entirely on liquid hydrogen and hydrogen-powered fuel panels. Another is the Super Eco Ship, which its builder, a company called NYK, hopes to have on the water by 2030. It would use a combination of solar, wind, and liquefied national gas (LNG) to power itself. Although these ships produce fewer carbon emissions than fossil fuels, a fleet of ships running on batteries or LNG could be harmful to the environment in other ways. Currently, batteries are made from a metal called lithium, which needs to be mined, or dug out of the ground. Lithium mining is very bad for the environment and has caused a lot of animal deaths. It also wastes a lot of water, which has caused shortages. To address this problem, some scientists are trying to figure out how to make batteries that do not run on lithium. However, as of 2021, they are a long way from a good solution.

This diagram shows how natural gas and oil are taken from under the ocean. Any problems with the equipment will immediately pollute the water

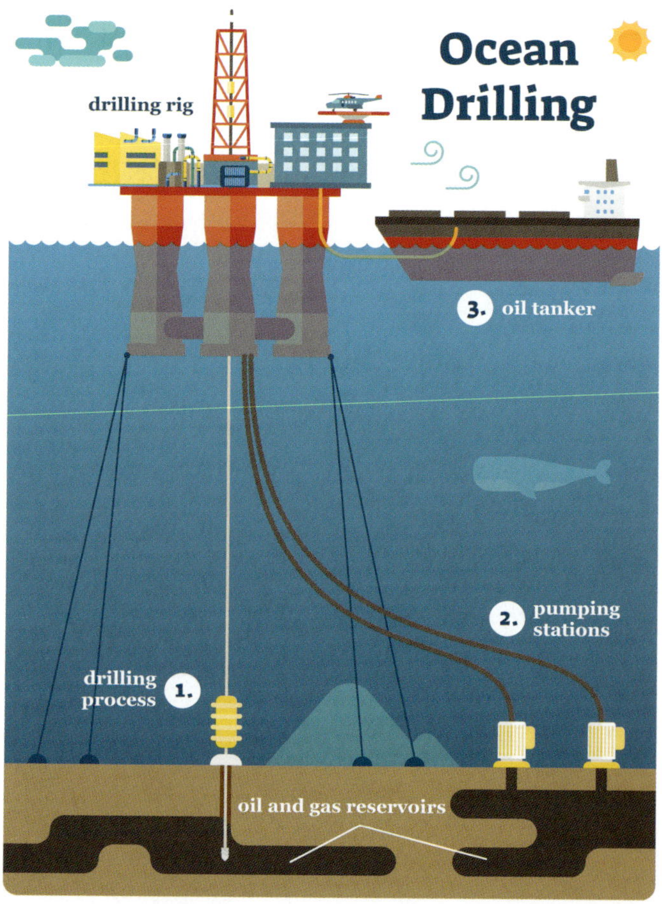

Natural gas also has problems. It produces less carbon dioxide when it is burned than gas, coal, or oil, but it still does produce some. It also releases a gas called methane, which is much worse for the environment than carbon dioxide. Getting the natural gas out of

the ground is often done through a process called **fracking**, which can also harm the environment. For example, it causes a lot of wastewater, which pollutes areas near where it occurs. Engineers have to think about issues such as these when they try to make ships eco-friendly, or better for the environment.

Some people believe the best option is to power ships with nuclear energy. The advantage of nuclear ships is that they can run for years on a limited amount of nuclear fuel, such as uranium. Nuclear power makes people nervous because it can cause big problems. Besides the issue of how to safely dispose of nuclear waste, there is also the risk of meltdowns. This is when the reactor gets too hot and melts, releasing the nuclear material in a way that can hurt or kill people. However, many supporters of nuclear power for shipping say that the smaller reactors such as those on ships are far safer than the big ones in nuclear power plants.

WHAT'S NEXT?

There are many technologies besides those that deal directly with fuel that will change shipbuilding in the coming decades. This includes programs that can help engineers and architects imagine what ships will look like. In 2015, *Marine Insight* reported on how the Naval Surface War Center (NSWC) used

3-D printing to construct scale models of a naval hospital ship. Such techniques can save valuable time and help eliminate poor designs.

Robots are on track to take over many dangerous and difficult shipyard tasks. Robots will also become more common on ships as crew members.

Yet another development that is still being worked out is ballast-free ship design. Many shipping companies and governments want to find a solution to the problems

Shown here is a model of what a floating city could look like in the future. Ships would transport people between the onshore city and the floating city.

ballast water causes when it is moved from place to place. Big, open pipes from the bow to the stern in the hull could let a ship's captain control water coming in and out without keeping any excess water inside the hull.

If the seas keep rising due to climate change, ships may soon become floating cities. In 2019, the UN put together a team with members from a private company called Oceanix, researchers from the Massachusetts Institute of Technoloy (MIT), and scientists from The Explorers Club. They came up with an idea for the world's first floating city, which they called Oceanix City. Like the *Prelude,* it would not technically be a ship because it would be anchored in place. However, if there are multiple floating cities, it is likely that people would use ships to travel among them. Only time will tell what the future holds for this ancient form of transportation.

THINK IT THROUGH

1. What jobs might robots be good for on ships?
2. What do you think is the best power source for ships?
3. Why might climate change make ships even more important in the future?

GLOSSARY

bow: The forward part of a ship or its hull.

breach: An opening made by breaking.

corrode: To gradually destroy or weaken.

dock: To haul or guide into a structure where ships are kept.

efficient: Able to produce a desired result with little waste.

emissions: Substances that are discharged into the air.

fracking: The process of injecting liquid into rock to extract gas.

invasive: Growing and spreading easily in a way that harms native species.

keel: The part of a ship or boat, sometimes finlike, that extends along its bottom to provide stability in the water.

knot: A measure of a boat's or ship's speed on the water.

maneuver: To move something in a careful and skillful way.

radar: A radio device for detecting the position of things in the distance and the direction of moving objects.

rudder: A flat, moveable piece of wood or metal that is attached to a ship and is used in steering.

stern: The back or rear-most part of a ship or boat.

turbine: An engine that has a part with blades that are caused to spin by pressure from water, steam, or air.

FIND OUT MORE

Books

London, Martha. *Military Ships*. Minneapolis, MN: DiscoverRoo, 2020.

Meister, Cari. *Boats and Ships*. Oxford, UK: Raintree, 2020.

Sirota, Lyn A. *Ships and Subs*. Mankato, MN: Black Rabbit Books, 2018.

Websites

FunKids: Sean's Ships—How Ships Work
www.funkidslive.com/learn/seans-ships
This website explains the science behind how ships float, move, turn, and more.

Kiddle: Sea Facts for Kids
kids.kiddle.co/Ship
A glossary gives the names of the parts of a ship as well as some different types of ships.

The National Maritime Historical Society
seahistory.org/kids
Learn about the history of sailing from the National Maritime Historical Society.

Organizations

International Maritime Organization (IMO)
4 Albert Embankment
London SE1 7SR
England
Email: info@imo.org
imo.org
The IMO is a group of 174 countries that work together to make international waters safer and cleaner.

Mystic Seaport
75 Greenmanville Avenue
Mystic, CT 06355
Email: info@mysticseaport.org
www.mysticseaport.org
This is the largest maritime museum in the United States. It is set up as a 19th-century seafaring village. Visitors can see the museum's collection of old sailing ships and talk to storytellers and historians in the village.

Tall Ships America
P.O. Box 1459
Newport, RI 02840
Email: manager@tallshipsamerica.org
tallshipsamerica.org
This organization teaches young adults how to sail replicas of historic ships.

Publisher's note to educators and parents: Our editors have carefully reviewed these websites to ensure that they are suitable for students. Many websites change frequently, however, and we cannot guarantee that a site's future contents will continue to meet our high standards of quality and educational value. Be advised that students should be closely supervised whenever they access the Internet.

INDEX

R

S

T

W

ABOUT THE AUTHOR

SOPHIE WASHBURNE has been a freelance writer and editor of young adult and adult books for more than 10 years. She travels extensively with her husband, Alan. When they are not traveling, they live in Wales with their cat, Zoe. Sophie enjoys doing crafts and cooking when she has spare time.